ROPE SPORTS

Ellen Labrecque

Raintree

www.raintreepublishers.co.uk
Visit our website to find out more information about Raintree books.

To order:
☎ Phone 0845 6044371
🖹 Fax +44 (0) 1865 312263
🖳 Email myorders@raintreepublishers.co.uk

Customers from outside the UK please telephone +44 1865 312262

Raintree is an imprint of Capstone Global Library Limited, a company incorporated in England and Wales having its registered office at 7 Pilgrim Street, London, EC4V 6LB – Registered company number: 6695582

Edited by Rebecca Rissman, Dan Nunn, and Catherine Veitch
Designed by Joanna Hinton Malivoire
Picture research by Ruth Blair
Originated by Capstone Global Library
Printed and bound in China by CTPS

ISBN 978 1 406 22693 5 (hardback)
15 14 13 12 11
10 9 8 7 6 5 4 3 2 1

ISBN 978 1 406 22700 0 (paperback)
16 15 14 13 12
10 9 8 7 6 5 4 3 2 1

British Library Cataloguing in Publication Data
Labrecque, Ellen
Rope sports. – (Extreme sport)
796'.046-dc22
A full catalogue record for this book is available from the British Library.

Acknowledgements
We would like to thank the following for permission to reproduce photographs: 11 (© Christian Pondella); Alamy pp. 6 (© Lonely Planet Images), 27 (© Jenny Matthews), 28 (© imagebroker); Corbis pp. 16 (© LAO CAI/epa), 18 (© Hitoshi Maeshiro/epa), 19 (© PATRICK SEEGER/epa), 20 (© moodboard), 21 (© Darren Staples/Reuters), 22 (© Louie Psihoyos/ Science Faction); Getty Images p. 23 (© Photodisc); PA Photos p. 17 (AP); Photolibrary pp. 9 (LOOK-foto/ Uli Wiesmeier), 10 (Flirt Collection/Don Mason), 12 (Oxford Scientific (OSF)/Mike Tittel), 13 (Robert Harding Travel/David Pickford), 14 (Blend Images/John Lund/ Drew Kelly), 25 (All Canada Photos/Keith Douglas); Shutterstock p. 4 (© EVRON), 5 (© Robert Fullerton), 7 (© Sean Nel), 8 (© Tyler Olson), 15 (© Curtis Kautzer), 24 (© Jonathan Larsen), 26 (© Matusciac Alexandru), 29 (© Artur Bogacki).

Cover photograph of a young woman hanging upside down from a bungee jump rope reproduced with permission of Getty Images (© Darryl Leniuk).

Every effort has been made to contact copyright holders of material reproduced in this book. Any omissions will be rectified in subsequent printings if notice is given to the publisher.

All the Internet addresses (URLs) given in this book were valid at the time of going to press. However, due to the dynamic nature of the Internet, some addresses may have changed, or sites may have changed or ceased to exist since publication. While the author and publisher regret any inconvenience this may cause readers, no responsibility for any such changes can be accepted by either the author or the publisher.

Some words are shown in bold, **like this**. You can find out what they mean by looking in the glossary.

Contents

What are rope sports?

This isn't a book just about skipping. This is the heart-stopping world of rope sports! In this world, people use ropes to jump off cliffs, scale icy mountains, and fly through the air!

! STAY SAFE!

Remember, these sports require a lot of training. Before you try one, train with **experts** first.

Bungee jumping

Bungee jumping is when a person jumps from a high **structure** while attached to an **elastic** cord. The cord stretches as far as it can, and then the person bounces back.

WOW!

Some bungee jumps are higher than 300 metres off the ground. This means that making bungee cords safe is very important.

Rock climbing

People rock climb on natural rocks or up human-made rock walls. A climber is tied to another climber with a rope. If she slips, her partner holds tight to the rope, to make sure she doesn't fall.

WOW!

Some athletes do not use ropes at all! This dangerous sport is called free climbing.

Ice climbing

Ice climbers use axes to battle their way to the top of frozen waterfalls, cliffs, and rocks. They are tied to a rope and **harness** for safety.

WOW!

In February 2010, Will Gadd climbed the frozen Hunlen Falls. The waterfall has a 374 metres drop – that's as tall as 87 double-decker buses stacked on top of each other!

Caving

Caving, also called spelunking, involves exploring deep, dark caves. Cavers use ropes to **descend**, or go down into a cave, and **ascend**, or climb up out of a cave.

WOW!

Some caves are found high up in mountains. Cavers must be good climbers to find their way into the caves!

Flying Trapeze

Do you want to fly through the air with the greatest of ease? Give the flying trapeze a try! A flyer leaps from a **platform** holding onto a trapeze, a bar hung by ropes. He or she swings back and forth and does tricks, sometimes with a partner.

Tightrope walking

Tightrope walking is the skill of balancing on a thin wire at a great height. Circus tightrope walkers perform in front of big crowds. Even more daring walkers travel between giant buildings and even mountains!

WOW!

Adili Wuxor, the "Prince of Tightrope", set a world record by spending 60 days living on the top of a tightrope in summer 2010.

WOW!

In 1974 Frenchman Phillipe Petit walked a tightrope between the World Trade Towers in the United States. These were the highest towers in the world at that time.

Tug-of-war

Tug-of-war is a game of strength between two teams. The world's biggest tug-of-war competition takes place every October in Okinawa, Japan. Each team has 15,000 people on it!

WOW!

The rope used in the world's biggest tug-of-war is 171 metres long and weighs over 36 tonnes. That is equal to nine elephants!

A rope course is a challenging outdoor maze made of rope. People have to climb or swing from one end to the other. The ropes can be set up on the ground, high in the trees, or on poles.

WOW!

Rope courses have been used to train soldiers as far back as the ancient Greeks in the 8th century BC.

Double Dutch

Don't be fooled. Double Dutch is tricky! It's a game where two long ropes are twirled in opposite directions, while one or two people jump over the ropes. Some even perform tricks while they jump.

WOW!

Double Dutch has a language of its own. *Patty Cake*, *Can Can*, and the *Spider* are all Double Dutch moves.

Rodeo

Rodeo includes activities such as roping and bull riding. In roping, a cowgirl or cowboy tries to catch a calf with a **lasso**. The winner is the one who captures the calf in the least amount of time. The calf is not harmed.

Be safe!

Rope sports can be exciting, wild, and thrilling. They can also be dangerous and scary. You should make sure you wear all the proper safety **equipment**.

Do not try any of these sports on your own. Listen to **experts** and have many lessons before trying extreme sports.

Get fit!

A strong midsection, or **core**, is important for succeeding in sport. Core strength is used for almost all movement, from jumping to running.

core

The plank exercise is good for making your core strong. Start with your stomach on the ground, and your hands right underneath your shoulders. Push up from your hands and raise your hips up in the air. Hold for 20–60 seconds each time.

the plank

Glossary

ascend move or climb up

Can Can Double Dutch move where the jumper gets his or her legs high into the air

core central, inner part of something. The core of the body is the stomach.

descend move or climb down

elastic able to spring back and forth

equipment tools or clothing that you need

expert person with a special skill or knowledge

harness safety equipment and straps used to support someone

lasso rope with a loop

Patty Cake Double Dutch move where jumpers clap each other's hands in a pattern while jumping at the same time

platform raised surface

Spider Double Dutch move where the jumper crosses his or her arms and places them behind his or her heels

structure something built or constructed

Find out more

Books

101 Youth Fitness Drills Age 7–11, John Shepherd and Mike Antoniades (A & C Black, 2010)

Living on the Edge: Bungee Jumping, Shane McFee (PowerKids Press, 2008)

Project X: Adrenalin Rush, Alex Lane (OUP, 2009)

World Sports Guide: Rock Climbing, Paul Mason (A & C Black, 2010)

Websites

www.bbc.co.uk/northernireland/schools/4_11/uptoyou/
This website has lots of information about healthy eating and exercise. Why not get fit and enjoy some extreme sports?

http://kidshealth.org/kid/stay_healthy/food/sports.html
Find out more about eating well and playing sports.

http://readyforten.com/skills/4-skipping
Learn some skipping moves to help you keep fit.

Index